The Emotional Lattice

How Patterns Form, Repeat, and Reorganize

Jennifer J. Moss, LCSW

The Emotional Lattice

How Patterns Form, Repeat, and Reorganize

Copyright © 2025 Jennifer J. Moss, LCSW

All rights reserved.

Published by Guiding All of You Publishing

No part of this publication may be reproduced, distributed, or transmitted in any form or by any means, including photocopying, recording, or other electronic or mechanical methods, without the prior written permission of the publisher, except in the case of brief quotations embodied in critical reviews and certain other noncommercial uses permitted by copyright law.

ISBN: 979-8-9939419-0-5

First Edition

Acknowledgments

The theoretical framework and clinical insights in this work emerged from years of practice, observation, and countless hours of reflection on what I've witnessed in the therapy room. I am deeply grateful to the clients who have trusted me with their inner worlds and taught me to see the patterns beneath the patterns.

I worked with Claude (Anthropic AI) as an editor throughout the revision process. The ideas, theory, and voice are my own; Claude helped me organize and clarify what I had already developed.

My deepest gratitude goes to my husband, Christian Pedersen, and my son, Nathan, for their unwavering support. They gave me the space and time to pursue this project, holding the household together while I disappeared into my work. Their patience and belief in what I was doing made this book possible.

I am also grateful to the Internal Family Systems community, whose work continues to deepen my understanding of the human psyche and has profoundly shaped my journey as a social worker, psychotherapist, and IFS practitioner.

Author's Note

I wrote this small book for people who sense that human experience is shaped by more than logic, time, or the linear stories we tell about ourselves. I don't mean mystical or supernatural - I mean deeply, recognizably human. It began as my attempt to understand what lies beneath those experiences—to offer a framework that honors lived reality without pathologizing, diagnosing, or reducing it to chemistry. Our inner world is layered architecture: memories echo in patterns, meanings cluster, and identity shifts in response to moments that feel connected across time. I wanted a model spacious, gentle, and clear enough for someone to say, *"Yes. That feels true."*

Here I explore three hypotheses—**Liminal Convergence, Harmonic Memory, and the Resonant Lattice**—that together offer a potential answer to "why is it like this?" None of these ideas ask you to believe in anything supernatural. They ask only that you notice what your own experience has already shown you: certain memories gather together, certain patterns repeat, and certain emotions ripple across the internal system in ways that can feel larger than they should.

This minibook is for anyone who has ever wondered why some experiences echo louder than they should, why unrelated memories feel woven together, or why one emotional message—often formed early—can feel like it covers the whole internal world. These ideas won't answer everything. But they might give language to the structures you've been feeling all along.

This is a theoretical framework, not a treatment protocol—a way of seeing, not a prescription for healing. If this framework provides even a little more understanding—or a little more compassion for the architecture inside you—then it has done its work.

— Jennifer J. Moss, LCSW

Introduction — The Architecture of Inner Experience

Human emotions and memories are layered, resonant, and interconnected. Thoughts, memories, emotions, and beliefs don't just accumulate; they form patterns shaped by shared emotional meaning.

Most of us have experienced a childhood memory so vividly that it feels as though we're right back there—when a tone of voice or story activates emotional reactions we haven't experienced in years, or when one passing comment stimulates memories we'd long forgotten.

A scent triggering a childhood kitchen. Your mother's phrase suddenly in your own voice. Feeling fifteen again in a work meeting.

A single repeated message—'You're always causing problems,' 'You're so stupid'—gathers across years, contexts, and parts. These emotionally similar experiences form what this model calls **harmonics**: clusters of memory that resonate together because they share a structural emotional pattern.

The feeling of being "too much" at age eight and at thirty-two. The familiar weight of disappointing someone, whether it's a parent or a partner. The sensation of bracing for rejection in a childhood classroom and a professional presentation.

But these clusters don't float in isolation. They interact through the internal architecture of meaning—what this model describes as **the Resonant Lattice**. The lattice is the internal connective tissue through which emotional messages travel, influencing parts of the system that may not share memories but can still feel their emotional tone.

This booklet presents a speculative cognitive model—a theoretical framework for understanding, not a clinical intervention. The model exists to help people understand why their emotional world behaves the way it does—not to diagnose or solve it, but to give language to what has always been happening beneath the surface. I explore three ideas: how convergence creates intersections, how harmonics structure memory, and how a lattice carries emotional patterns across the internal system. Together, they form a dimensional cognitive architecture that can explain much of what we feel, remember, repeat, and try to outgrow.

This model loosely aligns with traditions such as Jung's work on symbolic resonance and Lakoff & Johnson's work on conceptual metaphor, though it does not rely on them.

This is a conceptual framework—a map of how experience behaves from the inside. Throughout this book, I use "parts" to refer to the semi-autonomous aspects of our inner world, and "Self" to describe our core calm, clear presence.* The book explores the patterns inside human experience—how emotions cluster, how memories activate one another, and how meanings organize themselves.

*For readers unfamiliar with these terms: See the glossary at the end for a fuller explanation of Internal Family Systems (IFS) concepts.

Liminal Convergence: The State that Allows Access

Elena is in her mid-thirties when a coworker casually says, "You're so intense sometimes."

Nothing dramatic—just a passing comment—but it hits her with a heaviness she can't explain.

This is Liminal Convergence: a moment where present emotion blends with older layers, and several memories become perceptible at once.

Without knowing it, **Harmonic Memory activates**—a cluster of earlier experiences where she was told she was "too much," "too loud," and "too emotional," each carrying the same emotional tone of being unwanted.

Inside her, those memories don't feel separate; the **Resonant Lattice links them**, pulling distant moments into a single, unified emotional message.

That message surfaces instantly as a **global belief**: "I ruin things. I make people uncomfortable just by being myself."

Before she has time to think, her body is already bracing, apologizing, shrinking.

Later, when she revisits the moment gently, she realizes the coworker's comment was small—**the size of her reaction came from the size of the cluster**, not the size of the moment.

And knowing that doesn't magically erase the reaction, but it does begin to create a **shift**: she can now hold the experience with context instead of self-blame.

Liminal Convergence can be described as: the blending of boundaries that allows different layers of experience to temporarily coexist with each other. Sometimes, the blending can be so strong that the boundaries remain blended over long periods of time.

1. The Threshold State

Liminality is a transitional or in-between state. Liminal convergence describes moments when boundaries blur and intersect. A place where possibilities emerge from that intersection of different "in-between" phases—moments where the usual boundaries become intertwined. These moments can arise in reflection, exhaustion, prayer, meditation, awe, or during quiet tasks when the mind relaxes just enough to loosen its grip. These states, or moments, happen in many places and many times over.

In these states, layers of experience that normally remain compartmentalized begin to overlap. Thoughts blend with memories, emotions blend with symbolic meaning, and parts of us sense one another more clearly.

You're washing dishes, and suddenly you're seven years old and also thirty-five. You're watching the sunset, and grief from three different decades surfaces at once. You're falling asleep, and memories you thought were unrelated organize themselves into a recognizable pattern.

People often describe it like this:

"I suddenly remembered five things at once."

"It was like everything connected."

"I saw the pattern."

"I felt something from childhood and something from last week in the same moment."

This is exactly what Liminal Convergence predicts: layered experience becoming briefly perceptible as one resonant field.

2. Convergence as the Gateway

This model treats Convergence as the *access point* for the other two phenomena—Harmonic Memory and the Resonant Lattice—because:

You can't sense harmonics until the boundaries become blended.

You can't feel the lattice unless the harmonics activate.

Thus, Convergence is not the cause of emotional clustering—emotional similarity is—but convergence is the moment where you become aware of the clusters you already carry.

3. What is Convergence in this Context

When convergence occurs, the subconscious perceives emotionally-similar clusters. Harmonics—clusters of memories connected by emotional tone—which often go unnoticed in daily life because our internal system keeps them separated into different parts, roles, or timelines and live deep in the subconscious.

Convergence changes that.

It creates the conditions for:

cross-part emotional resonance

access to deeper memory patterns

sudden insight or recognition

"bigger than this moment" emotional reactions

multi-layered reflection

symbolic dreams or imagery

the sense of "many things shifting at once"

4. The Experience of Overlap

When two memories share a similar emotional tone, they often behave as if a small "portal" opens between them. A feeling in the present can suddenly activate a moment from years ago—not because the two events are logically connected, but because they vibrate with the same emotional frequency.

This doesn't only link events; sometimes it links parts of the internal system.

Some harmonics feel tied to identity—shadow-echoes of earlier selves or old roles flickering beneath the present moment. These identity harmonics don't always come with images or stories; sometimes they appear only as a mood, a posture, a mannerism, or a familiar internal stance.

If Convergence describes how emotional material becomes accessible, Harmonic Memory describes what that material is structured into once it becomes perceptible.

Harmonic Memory: A Clustering Mechanism

What if memory is woven together by emotional meaning or similarity?

1. Emotional Similarity as the Organizing Force

In this model, **emotional similarity** is the primary force that clusters memories together.

Events with similar emotional tones—shame, fear, tenderness, longing, joy—organize themselves into patterns. Emotional similarity is not only about feelings or tone—because sometimes the literal, factual content is itself the emotional pattern. When a person hears the same phrase—'dumbass,' 'too much,' 'stop crying,' 'you're impossible'—repeated throughout childhood, the emotional cluster forms not just from how it felt, but from the specific wording, the repetition, and the person it came from.

These elements combine to create a recognizable emotional signature. That signature can later be activated by different situations that match the felt sense, tone, and underlying message—even when the situations happen years apart, involve completely different people, are held by different internal parts, were forgotten or minimized, or might seem unrelated on the surface.

This is why the memory of a parent's critical comment can feel strangely connected to a boss's tone thirty years later, or why an adult conflict can feel bigger than it should. The similarity isn't in the content—it's in the **felt sense**.

Memory, in this way, behaves like a harmonic field: a structure where emotionally similar experiences "call to" one another and form clusters. Harmonic Memory describes how emotional similarity—not time, content, or logic—organizes experience into clusters that activate together and shape global beliefs. The harmonics spread *across and through* the internal system.

2. What a Harmonic Cluster Actually Is

If a child repeatedly hears, "You're too much," "You're too emotional," or "Stop being sensitive," those experiences do not store as isolated episodes. They bind into a harmonic cluster organized around the emotional pattern of **being overwhelming or fundamentally wrong for having needs**.

Later, a partner's sigh may activate the entire harmonic cluster, not just one memory. This cluster doesn't pop up as a memory but as an emotional reaction from a cluster of experiences in the subconscious. This is why the emotional response feels bigger than the moment.

A harmonic cluster is not a single memory. It is a **constellation** of moments that:

evoke the same emotional pattern

reinforce the same internal message

feel similar in the body

activate the same reactions or responses

carry the same, or similar, relational meaning

This cluster behaves like a **node**—a point of resonance that, when touched, activates many memories or emotions at once.

3. Cross-Part Harmonic Resonance and How Harmonics "Cover" Self

Take Elena: At seven, her mother snapped "You're too loud" at the dinner table. At fourteen, a teacher pulled her aside after class to say "You're too intense." At twenty-three, an ex-partner said, exhausted, "You're just *too much*." At thirty-five, a coworker said casually, "You're so intense sometimes."

These moments have nothing in common on the surface—different people, different decades, different contexts. But they share an emotional signature: *being fundamentally too much, ruining things just by being herself*. That signature binds them into a harmonic cluster. When the coworker spoke, Elena wasn't just reacting to that moment; she was reacting to the entire constellation.

Different parts hold different memories and burdens, yet can experience the same global belief—"I'm unlovable," "I'm unsafe," "I'm too much"—even though no single part holds all the memories. This happens because clustering occurs **within the lattice**, connecting experiences across the internal system.

For Elena, different parts hold different pieces of this pattern. One part carries the shame of the seven-year-old who learned to be quiet at dinner. Another holds the teenager's determination to never let anyone see her vulnerability again. A third manages adult relationships by preemptively shrinking, apologizing before anyone can criticize. Yet the message "I ruin things by being myself" doesn't live in just one part—it feels *totalizing*, as if her entire system has agreed it's true, even though no single part witnessed all those moments.

When certain experiences trigger a harmonic reaction, we react from the lattice lens instead of reacting from Self. This might be feeling inadequate or having impostor syndrome, feeling shame for "no reason," or becoming defensive without understanding why. In these moments, it isn't that the Self believes the message; it is that the lattice is broadcasting resonance throughout the internal system from emotionally clustered memories held across multiple parts and from many places in time. This doesn't allow that calm, courageous, compassionate self to respond. The lattice has overwhelmed or covered up Self.

This contributes to the formation of global beliefs, totalizing emotional states, disproportionately strong reactions to triggers, and the repetition of familiar patterns, while also explaining why healing can shift many things at once.

Harmonics function like internal constellations: touch one memory and others light up, each reinforcing the same emotional meaning. This is why a small comment can cause deep hurt, why a particular tone of voice can open a flood of feeling, why a minor failure can feel catastrophic, or why a song can awaken what feels like a lifetime of emotion.

4. How Healing Reorganizes Clusters

Healing is not about "reprocessing everything." It is about shifting the emotional structure of the harmonic cluster. When a core emotional belief changes—even slightly—the entire cluster reorganizes. This can feel like emotional lightness, sudden clarity, insight without effort, a shift in multiple memories at once, compassion emerging spontaneously, or the sense of "the story losing its grip." These experiences occur because healing is nonlinear and harmonics themselves are nonlinear in the way they reorganize.

Understanding Harmonic Memory is vital because it sheds light on why humans repeat patterns, why some relational dynamics feel inevitable, why triggers activate whole networks, why internal beliefs can feel globally true rather than situational, and why change can be both sudden and slow. It also helps explain why a single healing moment can ripple widely throughout the internal system. Harmonics may provide insight into the underlying architecture of emotional experience—not by presenting a solution, but by illuminating the structure that shapes how healing unfolds.

The Resonant Lattice: The Connective System

Harmonic Memory explains what clusters are. The Resonant Lattice explains how those clusters connect and travel through your internal system.

The lattice can be understood as the internal architecture that connects experience, linking memories, parts, emotions, identity statements, and symbolic patterns into a coherent (and sometimes incoherent) whole. The lattice is how emotional meaning travels.

You've felt the lattice. It's what you experience when a single emotion spreads rapidly through your entire system, when a belief feels universally true, when a tone of voice evokes a response far greater than the current moment warrants, when multiple memories arise simultaneously, or when a sense of inner truth emerges without being traceable to any one event. The lattice is the underlying architecture that makes these phenomena possible.

The lattice functions as both structure and process—the underlying architecture that holds these connections and the medium through which resonance travels. The lattice is a framework that describes how emotional meaning moves through the internal system—a network-like structure of associative, emotional, and relational patterning.

In this model, the lattice serves as the medium through which emotional propagation occurs. Harmonic clusters—groups of emotionally similar memories—do not remain isolated; they are linked across the system through pathways of internal meaning. This helps explain how cross-part resonance is possible even when parts appear psychologically walled off. Their memories can still resonate with one another, their emotional tones can synchronize, their messages can travel, and their burdens can influence the entire system. A child's shame carried by one part, a teenager's shame held by another, and an adult's memory of failure in a third are all connected through the lattice due to their shared emotional signature. This is the mechanism behind global self-beliefs: not necessarily a single part asserting "this is true," but rather an entire network broadcasting the same emotional tone.

Why Some Beliefs Feel Totalizing

Beliefs like 'I'm not enough,' 'I'm unsafe,' or 'People leave' rarely come from one part or memory. Instead, they emerge when multiple emotionally similar experiences accumulate across different parts of the system, each contributing to the same underlying emotional message. When these harmonics cluster, their tone is broadcast through the lattice, creating a felt sense of truth that appears global rather than contextual. The belief does not originate from one event; it arises from the cumulative resonance of many events that share the same emotional shape. Through the lattice, this tone permeates the system, which is why even after one part heals, the belief may still surface, why the message feels "everywhere," why no single memory seems to justify the intensity, and why individuals often cannot reason their way out of it. The message is not merely a thought—it functions as structural influence.

When Elena's coworker said "You're so intense," the comment traveled through her lattice almost instantaneously. The cluster activated. The lattice amplified the message across her entire system. Within seconds, her body was bracing—shoulders tightening, breath shortening—and the global belief "I ruin things" surfaced as if it were an undeniable fact about reality, not a broadcast from a decades-old harmonic structure. She hadn't consciously *decided* anything. The lattice had already responded.

Emotionally similar memories generate resonance within the lattice. Resonance means that activation in one area increases activation in others, allowing internal patterns to echo across the system. Emotional tones often move more quickly than cognitive narratives, symbolic imagery may become charged, and recurring patterns of thought emerge.

Healing, Self-Energy, and the Lattice

Self-energy remains present and intact at all times. Calm, curious, compassionate, and more. However, when parts become overwhelmed with an event or a collection of events, each part takes on a job of protecting the person by covering Self with protection. This process is similar to fog settling over a landscape: the terrain itself has not changed, but visibility is reduced. Just as fog does not alter the land but obscures what can be seen, a strong emotional lattice does not remove Self, but it makes access to it more difficult. When harmonics soften, the lattice communicates clarity; when they intensify, it generates distortion. As harmonics begin to reorganize, the system often experiences increased openness, and when they converge, there is access to insight. This is why healing frequently feels like the fog lifting—not because the landscape has changed, but because it can finally be seen again.

Healing, in this model, involves more than transforming individual memories or the experiences of isolated parts. It is the reorganization of the lattice itself—the shifting of the emotional structure that connects and shapes memory. This is why healing one moment often affects many others, why change in one part can influence the entire system, why a single insight can feel transformative, and why emotional or relational patterns suddenly loosen or realign. As the lattice reorganizes, symbolic imagery may change as well, reflecting the structural shift. Healing happens not just within parts, but between them—at the level of resonance.

How These Hypotheses Might Actually Be Useful

Here's how these concepts help explain confusing moments in daily life:

1. Why Small Events Feel Overwhelming

You're not reacting to one event, but to an entire cluster of emotionally similar experiences your system has carried. When someone triggers you:

the memory cluster lights up

the lattice carries the emotional tone across parts

the emotional amplitude intensifies

the present moment becomes infused with resonance from the cluster

The cluster is larger than the moment. When people say "You're overreacting," they misunderstand what's happening. This model gives you language for that experience.

The coworker's comment to Elena—"You're so intense"—was genuinely small. Casual, even. But it activated a cluster that included her mother's irritation, her teacher's concern, her ex-partner's exhaustion, and decades of learning that her presence was *too much*. The size of her reaction matched the size of the cluster, not the size of the moment. Understanding this didn't erase her pain, but it gave her something crucial: context instead of self-blame.

2. Why Patterns Repeat

Humans tend to repeat emotional patterns because harmonic clusters shape which relationships feel familiar and which dynamics feel "right" or "normal." They influence what feels safe—even when it isn't—and what feels threatening, even when it shouldn't. These clusters also affect how we interpret ambiguous situations and how we fill in the blanks of other people's intentions.

Marcus finds himself in yet another friendship where he gives everything and receives little. His friends seem loving at first, then gradually become unavailable when he needs support. He tells himself each time will be different, but the pattern repeats. What Marcus doesn't realize is that a harmonic cluster formed in childhood—when his needs were met with irritation or withdrawal—now shapes what feels "normal" in relationships. The Resonant Lattice highlights certain emotions, filters experience, gives weight to familiar meanings, and makes specific interpretations feel "true." When he meets someone emotionally available, they feel "off" or "too intense." When he meets someone who mirrors his childhood dynamic, they feel like home. The pattern isn't fate. It's structure. And when you recognize this, your patterns stop feeling like fate and start looking like structure.

This repetition happens because the lattice doesn't just organize what we remember—it shapes what we *notice*. When you carry a harmonic cluster around abandonment, you become attuned to signs of withdrawal in others—a delayed text response, a shift in tone, a cancelled plan. Your system scans for pattern matches. What might read as neutral to someone else registers as confirmation to you. The cluster primes you to see what it expects to see.

The lattice also influences what feels *safe* versus what feels *dangerous*. Familiarity often masquerades as safety, even when the familiar dynamic is harmful. A person who grew up with criticism might feel more comfortable with a critical partner than with someone who offers consistent kindness—not because they prefer criticism, but because kindness doesn't match the emotional signature their system learned to navigate. The unfamiliar feels destabilizing, even when it's healthier. This is why people sometimes describe feeling "bored" or "disconnected" in relationships that are actually stable and secure. The lattice is searching for the pattern it knows.

Breaking these patterns doesn't require willpower or forcing yourself into new behaviors. It requires recognizing the harmonic structure underneath—seeing that the pattern exists because your system is following an old map, not because you're destined to repeat it. Once you see the architecture, you can begin to work *with* the structure rather than fighting against yourself. The lattice can be reorganized. The cluster can integrate new data. The pattern can shift.

3. Why You Can "Know" Something Without Knowing Why

People often describe intuition as a sense—a knowing, a gut feeling, an immediate conclusion, or an emotional pull. This model suggests that intuition frequently arises from resonance: your system senses a pattern match, harmonics activate, and the lattice connects emotionally similar memories. In these moments, you *feel* the meaning before you can articulate the logic. This doesn't replace theories of heuristics or rapid inference; it simply adds the phenomenological layer. Intuition feels like resonance because it *is* resonance—the body and mind detecting similarity across time.

4. How Dreams Express the Lattice

Dreams are potentially one of the purest expressions of the lattice. When the conscious mind rests, the emotional architecture continues its work.

Dreams draw on harmonics, organize emotional clusters, express patterns symbolically, reveal cross-part influences, highlight unresolved or reorganizing material, and pull imagery from the lattice.

This helps explain why dreams can feel emotionally true even when they make no logical sense. The logic is harmonic, not narrative.

5. Why Certain Moments Heal More Than Others

Healing is nonlinear because emotional structures are nonlinear. A moment of genuine compassion, a new relational experience, a revelation, or even a simple felt sense of safety can shift a core emotional belief, reorganize a harmonic cluster, reduce resonance across the lattice, alter protective patterns, and clarify Self-energy.

A friend's unexpected gentleness. A therapist's steady presence during a memory. A partner saying "You're not too much" and meaning it. A moment of being truly seen without judgment.

When this happens, it may feel like lightness, relief, sudden insight, a loosening of old stories, clarity, or even a widening of internal space. These changes occur not because the mind is fragile, but because it is structured—and altering the structure of a single cluster can influence many things at once.

Months after the coworker's comment, Elena was working late with a colleague when she got animated explaining a project she cared about. She caught herself mid-sentence, bracing for the familiar response. Instead, her colleague smiled and said, "I love how passionate you are about this. It's contagious." The words weren't profound. But something in Elena's system *shifted*.

Not erased. Not fixed. But a new data point entered the cluster. A moment where her intensity wasn't *too much*—it was welcomed. The lattice registered it. The harmonic structure began, quietly, to reorganize. She noticed herself apologizing less. Feeling lighter in conversations. The global belief "I ruin things" didn't vanish, but it no longer felt like an absolute truth. It felt like an old broadcast losing signal.

6. Why Understanding Comes Before Change

Most people try to change behaviors, thoughts, or relationships without understanding the emotional architecture behind them.

When you recognize:

the cluster (Harmonic Memory)

the access state (Liminal Convergence)

the connective tissue (the Resonant Lattice)

…you stop blaming yourself for patterns that were never failures of effort—they were the result of structure.

This understanding creates relief because it restores context.

Bringing It All Together

Structure can change.

This is the premise beneath everything you've read. Your inner architecture is not fixed. It responds, reorganizes, and transforms.

Liminal Convergence explains why there are moments when everything feels connected.

Harmonic Memory explains why experiences cluster and repeat.

The Resonant Lattice explains why emotional messages travel across the internal system and become global beliefs.

Together they describe an architecture—not a solution, not a diagnosis, not a cure—but a **map** of how inner experience arranges itself.

Understanding this map doesn't fix everything. But it helps you see the path. And when you see the path, you can begin to walk it with compassion instead of confusion, with curiosity instead of shame.

Closing Reflection

Structure can change. You can change.

Your inner life is not random. It is not chaotic. It is not broken.

It is **architectural**.

Your memories do not simply sit in a pile—they cluster according to emotional similarity. Your parts do not exist in isolation—they influence one another through the shared structure of the lattice.

You are not defined by your patterns. You are shaped by them, yes —but structure can change.

You are not limited by your clusters. They formed in response to experiences you survived. They can reorganize.

You are not the global beliefs that sometimes cover you. Those beliefs are broadcasts from a lattice built during times when you had fewer choices.

You are more than your harmonics. More than your symbols. More than the emotions that echo across your system.

Self-energy sits beneath all of it.

Calm, clear, curious, compassionate—untouched by the clusters that tried to protect you or the messages that tried to shape you. The lattice may have carried difficult harmonics, but it is also capable of carrying relief, clarity, love, and healing.

This model exists for one purpose:

To remind you that the things that feel overwhelming or confusing often have a structure behind them—a pattern you can now see.

And what you can see, you can understand.

What you understand, you can hold with compassion.

What you hold with compassion, you can help transform.

You are not alone inside yourself. You are not chaos inside. You are a system—and that system can soften, reorganize, and come back into coherence.

There is beauty in that.

Where to Go from Here

Notice the moments of convergence. Get curious about your clusters. Be gentle with your lattice.

The simple act of seeing this architecture begins to transform it. You don't need to force change or fix yourself. Understanding itself is movement. Compassion itself is reorganization.

Trust that the map you now hold will reveal what needs to be seen, when it needs to be seen.

You are already on the path.

Epilogue: Patterns Across Deep Time

The core framework is complete. What follows is optional enrichment for those curious about how these internal patterns might express themselves across cultures and throughout human history. This epilogue explores the larger human story but is not essential to understanding or working with your own inner architecture.

Stepping back for a moment, we can see how this internal architecture could influence the symbols that appear in our dreams, myths, and cultural patterns.

Human beings across cultures and centuries have created myths, symbols, and stories with surprising similarities. These parallels do not require mystical explanations or collective consciousness theories. They emerge because core aspects of human emotional architecture are deeply shared.

We share the same nervous system, the same relational needs, the same vulnerabilities, the same longing, and the same fears. And so we recreate the same symbolic shapes.

By 'deep time,' I mean the long arc of emotional and symbolic patterns across human history and culture. If emotional patterns propagate through the lattice internally, we should expect them to echo externally—in the metaphors, stories, and symbols humans create. This outward patterning is not mystical; it is simply the way shared human emotional architecture leaves visible marks in culture.

1. Why Symbols Repeat Across Cultures

When emotionally similar human experiences cluster across individuals, they often give rise to shared symbolic patterns. These symbols mirror the emotional meaning of those experiences rather than the historical events themselves. The relationship between internal architecture and collective symbolism is not straightforward, yet the recurring parallels are compelling enough to warrant serious consideration.

Across cultures and lifetimes, humans return to images and themes shaped by emotional universals—loss, danger, separation, longing, betrayal, awe, rebirth, reconciliation, and protection. These recurring motifs emerge not because people share identical histories, but because emotional structures resonate across systems. When clusters of similar emotional experiences appear in different individuals, symbolic reflections of those experiences tend to surface in similar ways. The symbols become a kind of shared emotional language, echoing structures that feel familiar even when the stories that produced them differ.

Because these emotional states recur in all human lives, the symbols that reflect them also recur. Consider: Thresholds represent transition. Water represents depth, emotion, or surrender. Darkness represents fear or the unknown. Light represents clarity or truth. Descent represents overwhelm, shame, or crisis. Ascent represents empowerment or realization. Why do so many cultures use water as a symbol of emotional depth? Because the experience of being overwhelmed by emotion feels like drowning, like being pulled under, like losing footing in something vast and uncontrollable. The symbol emerges from the felt sense.

The symbols are not identical across cultures—their **emotional architecture** is. Healing reorganizes the connective tissue of meaning.

2. Symbolism as a Mirror of Harmonic Memory

Symbols are external expressions of internal clusters. When a symbol feels powerful, it often sits atop a large emotional cluster within your lattice.

Just as emotionally similar memories organize themselves through internal clustering, symbols tend to gather around emotional universals; myths cluster around shared human fears and hopes; and dreams form around the emotional logic of the moment. A descent into the underworld reflects the inner experience of entering a difficult emotional state. Likewise, a narrative of emerging into light is not about photons; it speaks to the experience of relief, clarity, resurrection, or realization. When emotional universals surface, they can activate symbolic universals, allowing the emotional resonance within the system to find expression through imagery.

3. The Lattice and Symbolic Patterning

The Resonant Lattice does not merely organize memories; it also organizes meaning. Symbolic thought is one of the primary ways humans make sense of emotional clusters, relational patterns, identity shifts, unresolved pain, internal conflict, and the underlying desire for coherence. When a symbol feels powerful or strangely resonant, it is often because it sits atop a large emotional cluster within the lattice. The symbol functions as a kind of shorthand—a concentrated representation of an entire emotional structure, sometimes holding layers of meaning that the conscious mind has not yet fully articulated. This helps explain why certain symbols seem to "follow" us throughout life, why some images feel meaningful without our fully understanding why, why dreams return to the same metaphors, why spiritual or mythological stories can feel intensely personal, and why some forms of art feel more like remembering than discovering. A person's symbolic landscape is not arbitrary; it is shaped by their emotional architecture. Symbols emerge where patterns hold emotional weight, acting as visible surface markers of deeper internal structures. When we notice which symbols persist, we are often noticing where the emotional architecture is still asking to be understood.

4. Patterns Across Individuals, Not Just Cultures

The recurrence of symbols is not only a cross-cultural phenomenon—it also unfolds quietly within a single life. A person may repeatedly dream of the same place, imagine the same image, feel drawn to the same type of story, or return to the same metaphors when trying to explain themselves. These repetitions are not evidence of fate or destiny, nor are they random. They emerge from the internal architecture of meaning—from the lattice. Symbols recur because emotional patterns recur. The internal system seeks coherence, and when an emotional cluster remains active or unresolved, the system returns to symbols that match its underlying shape. In this way, symbols function like resonant echoes: the mind reaches for familiar imagery not to circle endlessly, but to gesture toward something important—something it is still trying to articulate. They represent the emotional architecture calling attention to itself. The pattern persists until its meaning is recognized. Only then can it begin to reorganize.

5. The Function of Symbolic Universals

Symbolic universals help humans externalize internal structures, articulate emotional truths, find coherence amid complexity, navigate identity transitions, express what cannot be spoken directly, and feel less alone in their internal experience. They allow what is deeply internal—often implicit, fragmented, or impossible to language—to take form in a way that can be seen, held, and reflected upon. Symbols act as bridges between inner and outer worlds, providing a container for emotional meaning that might otherwise remain inaccessible or unprocessed. In this way, they do not merely illustrate experience; they help organize it. They function less as embellishments of the psyche and more as cognitive instruments—tools through which the internal system can recognize itself, communicate across parts, and move toward coherence.

6. Bringing It Together

In this model:

Harmonic clusters organize emotional experience.

The lattice connects those clusters into patterns of meaning.

Symbols emerge as representational echoes of these structures.

This is why certain myths, metaphors, and symbolic figures feel so familiar. They are not foreign creations—they are reflections of the same emotional architecture we all share.

Glossary: Internal Family Systems (IFS) Terms

Parts: In Internal Family Systems (IFS), a psychotherapy modality, parts function as semi-autonomous subpersonalities. They do not share full access to one another's memories or burdens, and often remain unaware of what other parts hold. Even so, parts frequently report experiencing the same shame, fear, relational insecurity, or a shared belief of not being enough. A part does not need to know another part's history to feel the emotional tone generated by another part; parts can feel the system and what's happening in it, and then respond in their own way with intense emotions and reactions.

Self/Self-energy: Self-energy is the core of who you are—calm, curious, compassionate, clear, courageous, connected, confident, and creative. It remains present and intact at all times, though it can be obscured by protective parts.

Appendix — Notes on Metaphor and Model Constraints

This appendix is included for readers who want deeper clarity on how to interpret the terms used throughout this work. It does not introduce new concepts—rather, it provides guidance on how to think about the model.

1. Dimensions

"Dimensions" in this model describe **organizational domains** within human experience—categories of pattern behavior.

2. Harmonics and Clusters

"Harmonics" refer to **emotionally similar memory clusters**, often distributed across parts. They are grounded in psychological pattern recognition, associative activation, and emotional tagging.

3. The Resonant Lattice

The lattice is the **connective tissue of meaning**. It blends elements of associative networks, schema theory, identity formation, and parts-based organization.

4. Resonance

"Resonance" describes the tendency of emotionally similar memories to activate one another.

5. Limits of the Model

This framework does not attempt to:

replace neuroscience

prove psychological theories

resolve trauma

map the subconscious

offer clinical diagnosis

It offers a conceptual way to understand:

internal patterns

emotional clustering

symbolic meaning

the propagation of emotional messages

moments of convergence

shifts in identity

The purpose of this model is clarity, not certainty.

At the end of the day, these ideas are a way of making sense of the things we feel but cannot always explain. They are an invitation —to notice. To pay attention to the subtle ways meaning weaves through our lives, and to consider that the patterns inside us may be more alive, more connected, and more responsive than we once imagined.

About the Author

Jennifer J. Moss, LCSW, is a psychotherapist who utilizes Internal Family Systems (IFS) in her practice. Her work focuses on helping people understand the emotional architecture beneath their patterns, without pathologizing or reducing human experience to diagnosis. This minibook emerged from years of clinical observation and a desire to offer language for what clients already sense about their inner worlds.